"If you want to live the life you've c
Dreams". Marilyn had to go throug
dream life—she can help you attain

~ *Jack Ca*
"Chicken Soup for the

"At last. The book you've been waiting ～ ～ and a dif-
ference in this world—and still have a ～～. In this slim and powerful volume,
Marilyn Tam, former President of Reebok and CEO of Aveda, tells how she
traded burnout for a life of Dynamic Balance. By following the simple and
brilliant guidelines she suggests, you too can make the shift to living the life
of your dreams."

~ *Joan Borysenko, Ph.D., NY Times Best selling Author of
"Inner Peace for Busy People" and "Fried: Why You Burn Out and
How to Revive", co-founder and former director of the
Mind/Body Clinical Center, Harvard Medical School.*

"Marilyn Tam speaks from integrity and life-long experience in our struggle
to achieve the universal dream of a fulfilling, meaningful life. Her Eastern
background and Western accomplishments create a voice that will resonate
with your life as well, and give you a fresh perspective on how you can improve the quality of your life, work and relationships."

~ *Mark S. Albion Ph.D., NY Times Best Selling Author,
"Making a Life, Making a Living", former Harvard Business School
professor and Office of the President, Babson College*

"In this useful and charming book, Marilyn Tam shares her secret formula for
creating the life of your dreams. As a former VP of Nike, President of Reebok
and CEO of Aveda, Marilyn takes you through the practical steps to achieving
a great life so you finally can just "Do it!"

~ *Arielle Ford best selling author of
"The Soulmate Secret" and relationship expert*

Marilyn Tam's book lifts us out of the paradox of "self-help" books that, instead
of simplifying, too often add to the ever-increasing maze of specialization and
complexity. Taking responsibility for our own healing and happiness should
not create more stress! As Marilyn shares her own story with truthfulness and
vulnerability, a series of intuitively productive practices unfolds. Marilyn's
genius for solutions takes second place only to her capacity for reminding us
how to ask ourselves the right questions, again and again, until the answers
take root within our own soul.

~ *Barbara E. Fields, Ph.D. Executive Director, Association for Global
New Thought; Co-founder and Director, Gandhi King Season for
Nonviolence; Program Director, centennial celebration of the
Parliament of the World's Religions*

Living the Life of Your Dreams

The Secrets to Turning Your Dreams into Reality

With tips from Jack Canfield, Joan Borysenko and other experts who are living their dreams today.

by

Marilyn Tam

Waterside Productions, Cardiff, California

SELF HELP/SUCCESS

Published by Waterside Productions Inc.
2055 Oxford Ave., Cardiff, CA. 92007

Copyright © Marilyn Tam, 2011
All rights reserved
No part of this book may be used via print or Internet or any other means without the permission of the publisher. It is illegal, unethical and punishable by law to use the material without approval. Brief quotes may be used in critical reviews and articles. We appreciate your support of the author's rights.

Print:
ISBN 13: 978-1-933754-77-2
ISBN 10: 1-933754-77-x

eBook ISBN
ISBN10: 1933754761
ISBN13: 9781933754765

For information about the book or other information about this title please contact Waterside Productions Inc. www.waterside.com

Another book by Marilyn Tam – "How to Use What You've Got to Get to Get What You Want" ISBN 1588720772•

Printed in the United States of America

Contents

Preface	7
Chapter 1 This Is Not the Life I Thought I Was Living	9
Chapter 2 Up Turn, Down Turn, Your Turn	14
Chapter 3 Life Purpose—Yours	20
Chapter 4 One Step at a Time	30
Epilogue	38
Family Photo	40
Reference Material	41
About Marilyn Tam	42
Acknowledgements	44

Preface

You wake before the alarm, turn over and then it hits you—you are already behind on what you have to do today. Out of bed you rush to get ready, grab something to eat, gulp down some coffee and *zoom* your nerves are already vibrating at hyper speed. At the end of the long and exhausting day, you fall into bed bone-tired and weary, feeling that you didn't accomplish many of the things you had to do, much less the ones you wanted to do. Sigh, is this the life I was born to live, you wonder.

No! **You have a choice; you can live the Life that You've Dreamed of Living.**

"Hah", you say, "What is that? I would settle for having a life! "Yes, I understand, I have been there. I know the edgy, nagging feeling, which gnaws at your insides and buzzes in your brain as you juggle more demands than humanly possible. There *is* another way and I am delighted to share with you how. Come with me on this journey to discover and fulfill your birthright—to live the life that you've always wanted.

I did not come from privilege. My early years were hard and I had a good number of devastating challenges in my later years too. However those are the very things that I give thanks for—my "training" gave me the understanding, insights and skills to achieve a life, which surpasses my wildest dreams.

I am the second daughter in a traditional Chinese family and my birth was followed quickly by the birth of three younger brothers. To say that I was unwanted would be an understatement—my mother left me in the hospital and had to be called to pick me up. My inauspicious entry into the world foretold years of physical and mental mistreatment. Rising from an abusive childhood to leaving my home in Hong Kong as a teen for University in America alone, to becoming a global business leader and humanitarian, I've found the secrets to achieving a life better than I've ever dreamed was possible—and you can too.

Now I live in Santa Barbara, California, walking distance to the ocean and the mountains, sharing a sunny, spacious and cozy home with the love of my life. I have retired from the corporate executive world to run my global speaking and consulting business and the non-profit charitable foundation I co-founded, from my home office.

As I look up from my home office, I see trees laden with ripening oranges, lemons and avocados in my organic garden, while the roses in the flowerbeds are vying with them for abundance and glory. On the other side, the pool is glistening in the sunlight, white and yellow plumeria flowers are wafting their sweet scent, the palm fronds and bamboo leaves are fluttering gently while the hummingbirds hover over the geraniums, lilies and irises in front of the little meditation house. Ah, indeed I am so thankful for my life. It is from this place of gratitude that I am writing this—for you, so that you too can have the life you want and deserve. **A dynamically balanced, happy and healthy life.**

Chapter 1

This is not the Life
I Thought I was Living

Born into a very traditional Chinese family in Hong Kong, I was the second daughter of parents who were desperate for a son. Then my mother gave birth to three boys and cemented my position at the bottom of the totem pole. With three younger brothers I grew up an unwanted, neglected and abused child in a culture where dirt was more valuable than a useless second daughter.

My one blessing was the name given to me by my grandfather. A very unusual honor for a Chinese girl, he named me Hay Lit after two respected Chinese emperors. This proud name empowered me to grow up believing that someone in my family cared about my future and inspired me to think that one day I could do something important with my life.

I knew there were other children who were much worse off than I. One of my schoolmates and her family of five lived in a single room where they shared a kitchen and bath with two other families. With both parents working, my friend still didn't have proper clothing or enough food to eat. It didn't seem fair that she had to live this way. At the age of eleven, I knew that making a positive difference and helping people in need was my true destiny.

As a teenager, I came to America alone for a college education. I was driven to make a positive difference in the world. Working my way through school, I completed my undergraduate studies and earned a masters degree in a total of a bit over four years. From the bottom of the totem pole, I climbed to the top of the corporate ladder in high-level executive positions at well-known international companies (V.P. Nike, President Reebok Apparel & Retail Group, CEO Aveda Corp.). Then I became an entrepreneur, a published author ("How to Use What You've Got to Get What You Want", is now in several languages), and co-founded a nonprofit organization (Us Foundation) dedicated to promoting the highest common good for humanity and the planet.

Along the way, I never forgot my true life purpose. As an executive in the apparel and footwear industries, one of my proudest accomplishments was helping to create positive change in the labor standards for workers in developing countries. Today, in addition to running my Foundation, I speak and consult with global companies and governmental organizations on leadership, diversity, life balance and other business issues and also help clients around the world enjoy productive balanced and healthy lives.

Then one day, my sister, who lives in Vancouver, B.C. called and said that she wanted to come to California and spend Christmas with me. "I'm sorry," I heard myself say to my sister who I dearly love and hadn't seen for over two years, "but I'm just too tired to even think about the holidays. In fact, I'm going to cancel Christmas entirely this year."

Listening to myself, I thought, "What am I saying? This is just ridiculous! This is crazy!" I suddenly realized that giving so much to help other people, I had completely forgotten about taking care of my personal needs. The truth hit me like a ton of bricks. I was shocked and embarrassed. My own labor standards were completely out of balance! The second daughter, Hay Lit, had been putting *herself* at the bottom of the totem pole.

My sister was speechless at first, but then she understood that I was just so burned out. I explained that my priorities were all mixed up. Because I had been giving everything I had to other people and to so many worthy causes, at the end of the year I had nothing left for me or my own sister!

Travelling around the world I had been teaching business and governmental leaders to honor their physical and emotional health, spend time with family and friends, and pursue their intellectual interests and spiritual calling. But I had not made time to do many of these things. Could pushing oneself beyond her limits into a state of total exhaustion be an example of low self-worth, self-neglect or even self-abuse?

Reflecting upon how the role of women in America has changed, I realized that today we are expected to wear many different hats—daughter, wife, mother, friend, career woman, and community leader. Juggling all these things, we struggle to stay in shape, look beautiful, have a spiritual core and become self-actualized—other expectations that we, as well as society have placed upon us. Every now and then, we have to stop ourselves and ask, "Am I taking care of the most important person in the world?" That would be you because without oneself, there is no way you could do anybody else any good.

Keeping all the traditional roles, women of our generation have taken on many additional responsibilities. Multi-tasking comes naturally to the feminine gender, leading us to believe that we can do everything, all the time, and all at once. But this is impossible, and sometimes in order to achieve what's critical and to remain sane, we just have to say no.

Whenever you feel overwhelmed, stop, take a deep breath, and then take another one, and then say, "What would happen if I didn't do this task at this very moment? What is really most important? What is the truth here for me? Pull yourself back enough to get distance and perspective. Listen to the voice of your inner wisdom. The answer will come.

In order to stay true to my life purpose, I have learned to put my own needs high on the list of priorities and practice what I preach. Only by striving to make certain that my life is sustained in a balanced way can I make the positive difference that is my destiny.

After all, how can I help to heal the world if I can't take care of me?

And you? Are you neglecting yourself to take care of others? Is that really working for you and your loved ones? When you are giving is from *lack*—it's unsustainable and will eventually not only drain you but also destroy the very relationships and structures you are working so hard to build.

Stop, take a deep breath, again, and repeat the above instructions as needed. Remember that you are part of the whole—if you neglect/abuse yourself and become a hole—instead of a valuable part of the whole—the whole will also have a hole.

Yes I know the bills have to be paid, the work assignment and laundry done—somehow all *will* get done. Believe me, it will. Continue to read with me please, this book will show you the way.

Chapter 2

Up Turn, Down Turn, Your Turn

For a long time it had seemed to me that life was about to begin—real life. But there was always some obstacle in the way. Something to be got through first, some unfinished business, time still to be served, a debt to be paid. Then life would begin. At last it dawned on me that these obstacles were my life.

~Fr. Alfred D'Souza

Do you often say: "I'll do that when _____ and the "when" is all about someone or something else? I'll _____ when work is less busy; when your parent/child/spouse/partner/friend demands less of you, or when there is more time or money so that you feel OK about allocating any for your own needs. The cause may be very noble; you are dedicated to your passion, to your family, to your job etc. The running theme is that someone or something else takes precedence over your personal needs. Your work, family, friends, community, and/or your humanitarian work have priority in your life over you. It/they are demanding more than you have to give and its seems that even that is still not enough.

Many people die with their music still in them. Why is this so? Too often it is because they are always getting ready to live. Before they know it, time runs out.

~Oliver Wendell Holmes

We read regularly about the Up Turn and Down Turn in the economy. When is it Your Turn? Your Turn is NOW. Time to take care of you. Wait, you say, what I am doing now is very important, if I don't do it, things will fall apart! I say if you continue this way, **You** will fall apart. Or maybe you already feel like you are crumbling inside and that is why you are reading—welcome, you have come to the right place.

> *When I am anxious it is because I am living in the future.*
> *When I am depressed it is because I am living in the past.*

~Author Unknown

Joan Borysenko, Ph.D. in her book, "Fried, Why You Burn Out and How to Revive" [1] devotes much discussion to this very topic. You can only perform optimally and take care of others when you are feeling properly nourished, physically, mentally, emotionally and spiritually. When we are efforting and giving with little consideration of our own needs, we burn out. Dr. Borysenko speaks about the Yerkes-Dodson law, which outlines the relationship between stress and burnout. The inverse U curve of stress vs. productivity, with productivity on the y-axis (vertical line) of the graph and stress on the x-axis (horizontal line) shows that the initial positive correlation between stress and productivity becomes an increasing hindrance to further productivity and growth after a point. You have to work a lot harder and still get less work of a poorer quality done when that threshold of stress has been exceeded—and eventually

---

1 Joan Borysenko Ph.D. *Fried, Why You Burn Out and How to Revive*, Publisher, Hay House

burnout occurs and life becomes mundane and meaningless to say the least.

Dr. Borysenko cites the work of psychologist Herbert Freudenberger and how he defines burnout—"the extinction of motivation or incentive, especially where one's devotion to a cause or relationship fails to produce the desired results". Does any of this sound familiar? I know it does to me, I've experienced it more than once and that is why it is my passion to share what I have learned in my journey back to a dynamically balanced, rich and joyous life with you.

Many women are living on the edge of their capacity, especially women with children. Working Mother magazine did a survey in 2010, which showed that many working mothers, who appear to be in total control, are actually under severe stress. 40 percent of the respondents drink heavily to cope with stress and 57 percent reported they have misused prescription drugs. And both of these figures look set to rise, Suzann Riss, Working Mother's editor-in-chief says.

It is not just working mothers but all women are feeling stressed and relatively less happy and fulfilled than before. There are many large-scale studies on happiness of men and women nationally and internationally and the sad fact is that women all over the world are experiencing less joy and more burdens.

The United States General Social Survey has done an annual happiness survey since 1972 on a representative sample of men and women (about 50,000 people so far) of all ages, education levels, income levels, and marital status: "How happy are you, on a scale of 1 to 3, with 3 being very happy, and 1 being not too happy?"

One of the most notable results is that women's overall level of happiness has decreased—compared to where they were forty years ago, and to men. And the drop is regardless of their financial position, martial status, any children, age or race. The lone exception is that African-American women are now a little happier than in the beginning of the survey in 1972, but they are still less happy than African American men.

Other countries show the same trend—the British Household Panel Study, Eurobarometer Analysis (15 countries) and the International Social Survey Program (35 developed nations) all point towards this same concerning fact. Women are feeling more and more unhappy in the past few decades and it is a global phenomena.[2]

There are many numbers crunchers and social scientists, who have more diligently combed through the many studies and statistics than I will ever do. The consensus from all their work is inconclusive as to why women aren't happier—it appears that economically, career-wise, socially, financially and relationship-wise that women have made significant headway since the studies first started tracking happiness. How is it possible that women are falling behind in happiness absolutely and relatively?

May I postulate an answer? That even though statistically all major factors in a woman's life seem to have

---

2 For more information, see Marcus Buckingham's book "Find Your Strongest Life", Publisher, Thomas Nelson

improved, the recent (last 30 plus years) expectations of a woman's role have been bolted on to the old stereotypes of a woman's traditional role. We women are now expected to perform dual stereotypes—the traditional daughter, wife, mother, homemaker and community service volunteer is now also supposed to be a career woman, well versed in economic, political and social affairs, exercise, eat right, look good, have a loving relationship with a suitable (attractive and wealthy) mate, a meaningful spiritual life and make it all look easy in the process! We have bought the image society has created for us, and most women struggle valiantly and vainly in our own ways to fulfill them. No wonder women are unhappy; it is an impossible list of accomplishments for anyone to achieve without burning herself up in trying.

Men have it a bit easier, but just a little: they are less tied to the traditional men's roles now and they are allowed to show their feelings more but they are now also expected to be more rounded in their pursuits—help out more around the house, be more of a father and yes, work on their physical, emotional and spiritual sides too. For some men this is a daunting list. Welcome to the new world where the media has raised the expectations of what each person is supposed to achieve to the level only possible in the fantasy land of commercials, movies, TV and the internet.

> "Nobody can go back and start a new beginning, but anyone can start today and make a new ending."
>
> Maria Robinson

OK, how do you start to get out of dangerous stress and into some semblance of dynamic life balance? First by acknowledging that there are just too many things on your plate. Then review your options and allocate attention and resources according to how you value each area of your life. I've often been asked when I give talks around the world, "Can you have it all?" To many in the audiences, it seems that I have it all and I have to laugh and say:

"Yes, you can have it all but not usually all at the same time."

It is all about priorities. In the next chapter we will discuss how to find your life mission. When you know your purpose for being alive; it is easy to judge the relative importance of every demand on your emotional, physical, financial and spiritual energies.

"A rock pile ceases to be a rock pile the moment a single person contemplates it, bearing within the image of a cathedral."

Antoine de Saint-Exupery

Chapter 3

Life Purpose—Yours

These are the two most important days in your life:
The day you were born
The day you found out why you were born

A humanitarian upon receiving an award for his work

Do you remember your dreams from when you were a child? You wanted to be some type of hero—someone who was inspiring for you—a cartoon character, a TV personality, a figure from a story book, an inspiring family member or some magical creature that could miraculously transform your surroundings to the happy, fun place you hoped it would be. What happened to that dream?

Chances are it was squashed by other people's expectations of you. "What are you going to be when you grow up? The acceptable answer usually was what they wanted to hear rather than what you felt was your life calling. You were supposed to be responsible; doing something that they felt was proper and right for you. Your own hopes, dreams and talents were almost an afterthought to them in many ways. They were seeing you through the lens of their own conditioning. Oftentimes what they wanted you take on was what they did or didn't do; it had much more to do with their hopes and fears than yours.

Then there is the media—glamorizing certain roles—movie and TV stars, athletes, rock stars, major business moguls and the rich, indulged children of people with enormous wealth and other unrealistic role models. These celebrities seemed to live charmed lives with little accountability and with nothing as mundane as bills to pay, dishes and laundry to do. Those subliminal messages crept into your mind, burrowed in deep and came out whenever you had a setback in your life—they made you feel inadequate, wanting and unhappy.

Bombarded by the relentless conditioning of what you are supposed to be, you packed your own dreams away; so hidden that you may have forgotten that you ever had them. You adopted the message that society gave you—you have to be rich, famous, multi-talented, beautiful and in good physical shape to be happy. Of course you also have to be accomplished in a profession, keep a beautiful home, have well behaved and smart children, be self actualized, spiritual, do community service and give back to the world. Oh, and you need to have the right i.e. rich, glamorous and good-looking partner on your arm to complete the picture. No wonder you may be confused as to your life mission!

I don't think I have ever worked in my life, because work to me means that you are really doing something you don't like.

John Kluge, multibillionaire founder of Metromedia

Maybe you are one of the fortunate who found their life purpose early and have stayed the course all your life. I am blessed to say that I am one of them. How do you find your reason for being? In my case it was through the realization that the world is a lot bigger when I am open to seeing from other people's perspectives.

At seven years old I was shunted off to live with my aunt and uncle in hopes that they would adopt me. They had no children after many failed attempts and my parents had two daughters and three sons already. As the second daughter I was dispensable and in fact, as my mother frequently reminded me, I was worthless.

Living with my aunt and uncle exposed me to people with more merger means who were happy and productive. They liked the freedom of their lifestyle of being outdoors and in nature, doing something they loved. My new family lived in a little fishing village and my friends were the poor fishermen children and the factory piecework children who I worked with. We assembled plastic flowers and embroidered needlepoint handbags at home or at special gathering places on the streets for pennies. Yet I was comfortable. No one told me I was useless.

Then life changed again. My aunt gave birth to their first child, a son. I was sent back to live with my parents again. This gave me an even sharper understanding of what it means to be unwanted.

School uniforms are great equalizers; we have no idea of the relative wealth of each other. Without distinguishing clothes we lose a tool that is often used to gauge/judge other people. Rebecca, one of my classmates turned out to be from a family of paltry financial means. With two working parents, my friend and her family lived in a room and shared a kitchen and bathroom with two more families. Often they didn't have enough to eat.

I was filled with outrage when I found this out. It didn't seem fair or reasonable that in spite all their best efforts, her family couldn't maintain the basics of life. I realized that no matter how bad my life may seem to me;

there are people who had it worse, much worse. No, not as some remote concept from TV, magazines or books (this was before the internet after all)—a real life person who I know personally is facing true hardship.

I vowed that I would grow up to help others attain what we all want—freedom from basic wants and happiness. My life mission was set—I was going to save the world. I was eleven years old.

It sometimes takes a defining event like my discovery of Rebecca's home situation to ignite the inner passion of what drives us. Other times your passion may be so hidden that you are not consciously aware of it yet. But everyone has one. Finding out what yours is will propel you to another level of existence. One in which you are motivated to do what you are destined to do.

Pursue Your Passion. We are all born with our own set of unique talents. We were put on this earth to serve a purpose and pursue what it is we are truly passionate about. Identifying, acknowledging, and honoring this purpose is perhaps the most important action successful people take. They take the time to understand what they're here to do—and then pursue that with passion and enthusiasm. Jack Canfield discovered long ago what he was put on this earth to do: how to inject passion and determination into every activity he undertook. Jack learned how purpose can bring an aspect of fun and fulfillment to virtually everything he does.

Jack Canfield's Mission Statement: "You have to believe it's possible and believe in yourself. Because

after you've decided what you want, you have to believe it's possible, and possible for you, not just for other people. Then you need to seek out models, mentors, and coaches" [3]

To have a life mission is to have a north point in your personal compass. It will guide you and help you determine the choices you make in every aspect of your life—from career, to friends, to how you choose to spend your time, energy and money. And your life mission is what you need to follow to bring you balance, happiness and inner peace.

How do you uncover your passion and life mission? First you have to trust that you have one—your own, not what others may have imprinted in your mind. Sometimes your true purpose is what you are already doing—if so, you understand and are at ease with the choices you have made in your life.

You feel happy, contented and dedicated to your chosen life path. Sure there are times when you are frustrated, and you temporarily forget why or what motivates you; that is natural for all human beings. You know who you are and what you are here on earth to do and be. Congratulations, you are one of fortunate ones on the planet. This book will help you address the "hows" so that you can be more effective in achieving your mission.

---

3 Jack Canfield, America's #1 Success Coach, is founder of the billion-dollar book brand *Chicken Soup for the Soul*© and a leading authority on Peak Performance and Life Success. www.freesuccessstrategies.com

For the majority of people, you may have some uncertainty about your life mission. Don't worry, you can determine it and strengthen it. Deep inside each of us there is a calling, a quest and hunger that we were born to satisfy. You can delve into your inner world and bring it out to guide your life. Here's how.

Your Heart's Prayer

Before you dedicate your life to a person, a marriage, a family; to a corporation, a political party, a peace campaign; to a religion, a revolution, a spiritual path; make one other dedication first. First dedicate yourself to LOVE. Decide to let Love be your intention, your purpose and your point. And then let Love inspire you, support you, and guide you in every other dedication you make thereafter.

Robert Holden

First find a quiet place where you feel comfortable and set aside at least 45 minutes of uninterrupted time for yourself. Have with you a pen or pencil and a writing pad. Yes, I know many of you write mostly on a computer but writing with your hand connects you more deeply to the core of your being. We are working to link you to your inner self. If you really have a difficult time with using paper and pen, use a computer the **next** time you do this exercise. Please, at least for the first time use paper and pen. You will be amazed.

Sit in a comfortable chair or on a cushion and settle down mentally into your quiet space. If you meditate, utilize that process now to facilitate an open mind. If you are somewhat new to meditation, here are a few simple steps to help you clear your mind.

How to Quiet the Mind:

1 Breathe in deeply and exhale emptying your lungs gently. Keep repeating this process and with each new breath notice the air going in and coming out of your nostrils.

2 Allow your awareness to extend to the rest of your body; notice how the rest of your body feels. Where is the air going? Do you feel more circulation and warmth in your body? Focus your awareness in the center of your body, a bit above your belly button. As you stay with the process you may sense your body gradually relaxing.

3 Continue breathing and observing your body's response. When a thought comes into your mind, let it go gracefully without judgment. Thoughts are going to arise; when you disregard them they will leave. It is only when we pay attention to them do they hang around.

4 Many thoughts may come and it could be a challenge to find that quiet space—keep the faith. Allow the thoughts to come and go, do not judge the thoughts or your ability to have a quiet mind. You will notice that it gets easier over time. Even long time meditators have less than perfect sessions. Be kind to yourself, that's a large part of what this is all about!

For some of us a repetitive physical activity like walking helps to still our minds. Mahatma Gandhi frequently went on walking meditations to complement his sitting meditations. Zen monk, Thich Nhat Hanh, developed a form of meditation based on this concept — it is named appropriately, the walking meditation. Find the method that best stills the mind chatter and gives you the mental spaciousness that invites your inner wisdom to surface.

When your mind is open, ask yourself the question—"What makes me happy?" Write down whatever comes to your mind. Keep writing. After the first several sentences you may find that you have some resistance—persevere and just put down whatever comes into your mind about the question. When you break through the block, deeper feelings will come through. Remember to continue to breathe deeply and stay centered in your body. Don't judge your thoughts; just jot them down. Journal for at least for ten minutes and if you have more, continue.

Then start on the next question: "How do you want to be remembered?" Repeat the above exercise. When you feel that you have exhausted the topics for the moment, close your eyes. Sense into your body again. What are you feeling? What images are coming to your mind? Allow yourself to review them as if you are an observer. With compassion ask yourself the questions—"Is there more that you want to say to me now? Anything else that is important for me to know?" Listen carefully to the answers.

Here is a short summary of the **Journaling Process to determine Your Mission:**

1. Create a quiet space for a minimum of 45 minutes
2. Prepare pen/pencil and paper and a comfortable place to sit to journal
3. Settle your mind—practice your meditation or do the above Quiet the Mind process
4. Freely jot down the thoughts that come to your mind as you ask the question—What makes you happy?
5. Write on the subject for at least 10 minutes
6. Keep breathing and stay relaxed without judgment
7. Ask yourself "What do I want to be remembered for?"
8. Journal on the question for at least 10 minutes
9. Close your eyes and mentally review the whole process—listen for the answers —write down anything that you want to add to your responses above.

Congratulations, you are now on the path to determining your life mission. Please note that this is a journey; we are in the process of uncovering something precious that may have been buried for most of your life. Whatever insights you get from the exercise will grow as you give it space in your mind. Repeat this process several times over the next few days and weeks until you have delved into the deepest desire you have—your very reason for being alive.

In the process of claiming your life mission, you will also be affirming the values that you hold dearest. Your values and your mission are the foundation for your life. Nurture them; use them as your assessment tools to make decisions. That will ensure you are living in accordance with what is dearest to you.

Each one of us was born to fulfill a destiny. When you uncover yours, initially it may be a soft resonating whisper. With nurture, it will act like your personal foghorn guiding you through any confusion and murkiness surrounding any important decision. You will find that you can see past the inevitable "obstacles" in life to the bigger picture of what is important.

Armed now with your life purpose, we are going to help you move forward to transforming your dreams into real life—the life that you are living.

> *I have come to the frightening conclusion that I am the decisive element.*
> *It is my personal approach that creates the climate.*
> *It is my daily mood that makes the weather.*
> *I possess tremendous power to make life miserable or joyous.*
> *I can be a tool of torture or an instrument of inspiration.*
> *I can humiliate or humor, hurt or heal.*
> *In all situations, it is my response that decides whether a crisis is escalated or de-escalated,*
> *and a person is humanized or de-humanized.*
> *If we treat people as they are, we make them worse.*
> *If we treat people as they ought to be, we help them become what they are capable of becoming.*
>
> Johann Wolfgang von Goethe, 1749-1832

Chapter 4

One Step at a Time

One step at a time is good walking

Chinese proverb

You're ready to do something about the overload and stress in your life; the question is where do you start?

There may be more than one aspect of your life causing you discomfort and anxiety—this is common in today's taxing world. Oftentimes the sore points are related to each other and aggravating other areas of your life. Whew, what does this mean? It just means that you are human and living in our modern hyper speed world—just recognizing and acknowledging the situation is already a step towards improving it.

Many years ago when I was vice president of Nike, I lived in Lake Oswego, Oregon while my husband stayed in Southern California for his work. Both our jobs were exciting, very taxing and could suck up all the time there was in each day and more. After nine months of long distance commuting, we were both tired and cranky when we saw each other. Our visions of enjoying our precious time together went out the window soon after we reunited because we were both worn out from the stress of working long, pressure charged days. Packing up and flying during the little free time we had to see each other and then having to pack up again after a day made our times together less than relaxing. We argued over petty little things and felt unappreciated by each other. It seemed that our relationship was breaking down.

Our physical and mental health were also affected. We didn't exercise as much as much as we used to since we were jamming all the demands of a week into five days so that we could be together the other two. When our physical body is out of sync, our mental health is also affected. Laundry, household chores, grocery shopping, bills, etc. somehow still had to be dealt with while more "important" things were calling for our attention. Piles of papers and unfinished tasks lying around reminded me of what I still had to do—it made me feel miserably inept. I felt especially bad when a friend or even worse, my husband or his children from a previous marriage would ask me for something and I couldn't respond in a timely fashion. My work was demanding and exciting; learning a new industry, company culture, and town/living arrangement while developing a comprehensive and innovative new strategy for an emerging apparel division for one of the world's largest athletic company is a tall order. I was being stretched so thin that I didn't even recognize that I was stretched thin!

I even contemplated spending more time at work and skipping more of our personal time because the work was so challenging. One visit around New Year's resulted in my husband leaving early to go back to California in a huff. It finally struck us that our priorities were out of order. It took that big of a jolt for us to realize that our work had taken over our lives.

Have you ever been there? You have so much on your plate that you are not even aware of the enormity of the problem. In many ways that is easy to do—we add one more thing to our lists of "to dos or ought tos" and we soldier on. The last obligation we took on may be a good or necessary one, but we never stopped to review and assess if there was anything or even several other things we could take off our plate!

> *We need to maintain a proper balance in our life by allocating the time we have. There are occasions where saying no is the best time management practice there is.*
>
> ~ Catherine Pulsife

Here's a little quiz to help you determine where to begin the whittling process— and the good news is that you already have the right answers. All you have to do is use your life purpose, which you affirmed in the last chapter, as your guide and answer from your heart and the correct priorities for you will be revealed.

Quality of Life Quiz
Rank and write about the quality of the following aspects of your life:

> Physical Health
> Mental Health
> Financial Health
> Career
> Family Relationships
> Personal Relationships
> Spiritual Health

Similar to how you identified and affirmed your life purpose in the last chapter; use the Journaling technique to figure out your next steps. I am outlining the Journaling process here again for your convenience.

Short summary of the Journaling Process:
1. Create a quiet space for a minimum of 45 minutes
2. Prepare pen/pencil and paper and a comfortable place to sit to journal
3. Settle your mind—practice your meditation or use the Quiet the Mind technique outlined in chapter 3
4. Freely jot down the thoughts that come to your mind as you think about each aspects of your life as listed above.
5. Rank and write on each topic for at least 5 minutes
6. Keep breathing and stay relaxed without judging your feelings and thoughts
7. Close your eyes and mentally review the whole process—listen for the answers —write down anything that you want to add to your responses above.

To a large extent, the various aspects of your life are interrelated. Please respond by sensing into each one to determine which one(s) are triggering discontent and problems in the other areas. Journal on each one and write down your feelings and thoughts about them one by one, for example:

Physical health—*"I'm overall pretty healthy but I am tired a lot and get neck pain and headaches. My health issues seem to come mostly during the week and on Sunday night. I wonder if my neck pain, headaches and tiredness come from my frustration at work where I am struggling to stay interested in what I do. It seems so meaningless as I have been doing the same thing for so long and it doesn't seem to make a difference..."*

The above is a composite of the remarks I've heard from people I've coached. In this example they are saying that even though their physical health may have some challenges, the underlying cause seems to stem from their dissatisfaction at work. When they rank and write about their work, this knowledge of the reason for their health issues will help them identify what is frustrating about their work. With new insight they can explore what they can do to improve their work situation so that all aspects of their lives are more in balance. For people with this profile, it would be most effective for them to start by reviewing their career and analyze what they are drawn to and what they wish to modify. They can then make plans to start the process of doing what it takes to change it.

Go over all the different aspects of your life and rank them and write about your satisfaction/dissatisfaction with them. When you are done, go back and read them again, add any further thoughts you have about each area.

Just as your car runs more smoothly and requires less energy to go faster and farther when the wheels are in perfect alignment, you perform better when your thoughts, feelings, emotions, goals, and values are in balance.

Brian Tracy

When you have identified the relative balance/imbalance in the various facets of your life, you are able consciously make adjustments that will help you come back into balance. Look at your list—one area or two will show up as where you focus most of your energy, and one or two other ones will be the most neglected. Before you jump in and make any drastic changes, measure these areas against your life mission that you identified in the last chapter. Is your life as you are living it now aligned with your life purpose? If so, congratulations, fine-tune your energy, time and other resources to reflect more of a balance in your life. Pay more attention to the areas most overlooked and dial back on the most heavily emphasized ones.

When I speak about balance, I mean **dynamic balance**. At different times in our lives, our priorities vary. Life is active and constantly changing, so do our particular needs at different stages. It is unrealistic and almost impossible as well as unnecessary to allocate the same amount of energy and resources to every aspect of your life. Each person has individual wants and needs that ebb and flow over time. Therefore balance is dynamic, what is right and comfortable for you when you are twenty five is most probably radically different from what is suitable and happy for you when you are forty five or fifty. You have to be aware and reassess and adjust your dynamic balance as your life situation changes. What doesn't change is your life mission, which is your constant guide and the north point of your personal life compass. Use your life mission as the criteria to assess your Quality of Life at various times in your life.

Most of us have unbalanced areas that are screaming for help and attention at every stage in life—

that is a byproduct of our natural life cycle changes. The relentless pace of life today heightens the intensity of discomfort and amount of change needed. Knowing your Life Mission will help guide you to allocating the proper amount of energy and attention to each aspect of your life. Dynamic Balance is what we strive for—we can't do it all but we can knowingly adjust the amount of our resources we dedicate towards each part of our life at each particular period. Being conscious about what we choose to do, we can get buy-in and cooperation from others much easier than when we are acting unaware. We can make purposeful decisions and plans once we are conscious of our true values instead of acting in reaction to outside events.

> The best and safest thing is to keep a balance in your life, acknowledge the great powers around us and in us. If you can do that, and live that way, you are really a wise man.

Euripides

Recently some fascinating finding of what keeps people healthy and living a long and happy life was released. A longevity research project which tracked 1,500 people from childhood to old age and death started in 1921 and is still ongoing. Howard S. Friedman, Ph.D. and Leslie R. Martin, Ph.D. published the results of this eight decades study in their book, "The Longevity Project". The results are enlightening:

> The people who worked the hardest lived the longest. Being involved in, committed to, and successful at work is an excellent predictor of health and longevity.

> Social relations are important to good health, but it didn't much matter if you felt appreciated; much more important was how much social involvement you had with other people each day.

Staying active in middle age was more important than being active or being an athlete in youth. In fact, if you gradually became more physically active as you aged, that was a very good sign.

Happiness is related to health but not because laughter clears clogged arteries. Rather, we found that same kinds of meaningful and consequential lives that promoted health also promoted happiness.[4]

As you review your priorities, chew on this information. What is of consequence to life is to create meaning, have social interactions that you value and to nurture your physical body. In my consulting work with high potential corporate and nonprofit leaders and in my own life, I find that one is most alive, healthy and successful when one is making a positive difference, taking care of themselves physically, mentally and spiritually and have loving relationships. You now know your Life Purpose and your Priorities; seize the moment, take the steps to gain your life dynamic balance and the life you've always dreamed of. You can start now!

Life is like riding a bicycle. To keep your balance you must keep moving.

Albert Einstein

---

4 "Howard S. Friedman, Ph.D. and Leslie R. Martin, Ph.D., *The Longevity Project: Surprising Discoveries for Health and Long Life from the Landmark Eight-Decade Study*

Epilogue

Congratulations on taking steps to achieving your dream life. You are now on your way. Do the Life Mission exercise and the Quality of Life Exercises whenever you feel stuck or confused about your priorities. Reviewing your reason for being can give you an energizing boost and keep you moving forward when you feel discouraged. An abundance of insights and wisdom are stored within you waiting for you to tap into them. My goal is to help you access that powerful source of intelligence. The list of reference guides, which follow this, is another resource; use them as further support for you on your life journey.

According to Kevin Hansen, founder of Secret Regrets, a website which allows people (over 10,000 and counting) to post their answers to that question—the overriding regret is what was not done—not taking a risk and now forever being tormented by the possibilities missed. Look at how you are living your life. Be courageous, dare to do what is needed to align with your life mission, there is much here to support you as you fulfill your dreams.

What you have read is the first four chapters of a larger book in progress, which will provide more specific information, support and tools for each aspect of your life. If you are interested in more information about when additional chapters and the complete book will be ready, please email me at info@HowToUseWhatYouveGot.com You can also read more about my work and the upcoming book on my website www.HowToUseWhatYouveGot.com Enjoy your dynamically balanced life!

Family Photo

Sister, aunt, and Marilyn

References

Life Mission

How to Use What You've Got to Get What You Want
Marilyn Tam Ph.D.; publisher SelectBooks

Fried, Why You Burn Out and How to Revive
Joan Borysenko Ph.D.; publisher Hay House

Tapping the Source: Using the Master Key System for Abundance and Happiness
John Selby, Richard Greninger, William Gladstone; publisher Sterling Ethos

The Success Principles: How to Get From Where You Are to Where You Want to Be
Jack Canfield, Janet Switzer; publisher Harper

The Longevity Project: Surprising Discoveries for Health and Long Life from the Landmark Eight-Decade Study
Howard S. Friedman, Ph.D. and Leslie R. Martin, Ph.D.; publisher Hudson Street Press

Man's Search for Meaning
Viktor E. Frankl M.D.; publisher Beacon Press

Making a Life, Making a Living: Reclaiming Your Purpose and Passion in Business and in Life
Mark Albion Ph.D.; publisher Business Plus

About Marilyn Tam

Marilyn Tam grew up to her mid teens in a traditional Chinese family in Hong Kong. She left home to come to the USA alone, without finishing high school, to enter University, which she completed quickly with a master's degree in Economics. Rejected by World Health Organization (WHO) because she did not have the requisite ten years of work experience to join when she graduated, she pursued a career in the corporate world and incorporated her humanitarian work into her everyday work and life.

She rose meteorically in the international business world to become an influential corporate leader, speaker, corporate consultant, author and respected humanitarian.

In her corporate career, she was successively vice president of Nike Inc., president of Reebok Apparel and Retail Group and CEO of Aveda Corp. Marilyn founded Us Foundation in 1996 to facilitate global action and dialogue on social, economic and environmental issues. www.usfoundation.org She is also an entrepreneur, developing and building four different companies—corporate consulting and training, a web portal, a supply chain software company and an integrated healthcare company.

She is a national Director and the Chair of the Nominations and Governance Committee of SCORE Association, a Partner of the U.S. Small Business Administration. SCORE consults with close to 500,000 businesses a year, staffed by over 13,000 volunteers in 378 offices.

Her first book, "How to Use What You've Got to Get What You Want", is published in English, Chinese, Japanese Spanish and Indonesian. In the book, she combines her business acumen with her passion for giving back, to guide others to achieve their highest potential and dreams. www.HowToUseWhatYouveGot.com

Because of her broad and powerful experience, Marilyn is sought after as an expert and speaker in diverse areas—from leadership and diversity to life balance and health issues.

Marilyn was recognized as one of the Top 30 Female Entrepreneurs in the USA by Fempreneur magazine. Jack Canfield detailed her work in his book on the strategies for success, "The Success Principles". She is featured in the best selling book, "Fearless Women, midlife portraits" by Alspaugh, Kentz, and Halpin among other books.

She starred in several documentary movies as an expert and inspiration for others, including: GLOW Project, The Compass, Tapping the Source, Vitality, The Lost Message and The Gratitude Experiment.

She has received many honors, including the Artemis Award for her business and humanitarian work by the Greek government and the Euro American Women's Council, with her likeness on a Greek postage stamp, a Lifetime Achievement Award from eWomenNetwork, and an honorary Doctorate from Old Dominion University.

"Living the Life of Your Dreams" is Marilyn's latest contribution to the wellbeing of all who wish to live their ideal life—the life we are all born to live.

info@HowToUseWhatYouveGot.com
www.HowToUseWhatYouveGot.com

Acknowledgments

Nothing I have ever done is my work alone—friends and family have added their encouragement, advice and support in many ways to make them happen. First I want to thank Bill Gladstone, my literary agent and friend for pushing me to write this book. Bill urged me to write about the insights I've learned in creating my dream life—a life better than I've ever dreamed of. I am grateful to be able to share what I learned along my bumpy journey to happiness and inner peace so that others may benefit from the signposts and short cuts I've found along the way.

For all my friends and family who have been there for me through the years; offering me a shoulder, insights and many laughs along the way. Deep thanks in no specific order to Tom, Jan, Henry, Barbara, Lailan, Sean, Alyce Faye, Candis, Jodi, Gueta, Glenn, Mark, Sophia and many other unnamed ones who have been so generous with your time, support and humor when I needed it.

For my mentor who passed away last year, Robert Muller, former Assistant Secretary General of the United Nations. Robert, your wisdom, irrepressible optimism and twinkling eyes will be sorely missed.

Keith Carlson, thank you for your steadfast and expert help on all things computer and Internet. You keep me current in today's electronic world.

Kevin, you inspire me, make me laugh and remind me that life is to be enjoyed every moment. Thank you for being in my life. My life is deliciously more joyously balanced with you in it.

Most of all to Spirit, without whom I am nothing.